Behind the Lines

Behind the Lines

Cartoons by Tony Auth

Houghton Mifflin Company   Boston   1977

Library of Congress Cataloging in Publication Data

Auth, Tony.
　　Behind the lines.

　　　1. Watergate Affair, 1972–　　— Caricatures and cartoons. 2. United States — Politics and government — 1969–1974 — Caricatures and cartoons. 3. United States — Politics and government — 1974–1977 — Caricatures and cartoons. 4. World politics — 1965–1975 — Caricatures and cartoons. 4. American wit and humor, Pictorial. I. Title.
E860.A94　　741.5'973　　　77-9395
ISBN 0-395-25789-1
ISBN 0-395-25946-0 pbk.

Printed in the United States of America

A 10 9 8 7 6 5 4 3 2 1

Most of the editorial cartoons in this book first appeared in *The Philadelphia Inquirer*.

Tony Auth's cartoons are distributed internationally by The Washington Post Writers Group.

To Sharon

I started drawing while confined to bed for a year when I was five. Radio serials and comic book characters were my principal sources of inspiration.

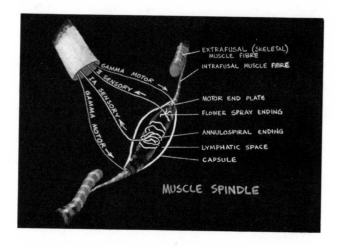

EXTRAFUSAL (SKELETAL) MUSCLE FIBRE
INTRAFUSAL MUSCLE FIBRE
GAMMA MOTOR
II SENSORY
IA SENSORY
GAMMA MOTOR
MOTOR END PLATE
FLOWER SPRAY ENDING
ANNULOSPIRAL ENDING
LYMPHATIC SPACE
CAPSULE

MUSCLE SPINDLE

My first formal training in art was at U.C.L.A., where I majored in Biological Illustration. After graduation I went to work as the medical illustrator at a large teaching hospital, where I drew charts and graphs and illustrated surgical procedures.

I was easily recognized in surgery.

I discovered the medical profession was thirsty for humor, so I began illustrating lectures with medical cartoons, such as this drawing from a lecture on skin care.

I became interested in politics because of the war in Vietnam. It seemed to me that the war was completely opposed to the interests of our country. As a result, I began doing political cartoons, which were published in the U.C.L.A. *Daily Bruin* and other campus newspapers.

'OK, so you want to end the war, end racism, end poverty, and end pollution. But what about something POSITIVE?'

4/12/70

"I've gotta stop smoking grass. It makes me paranoid."

1970

Four years later, I was hired as editorial cartoonist by the *Philadelphia Inquirer.*

PERSONNEL →

My typical day begins at 6 A.M. I must decide what I want to draw in time for the 9:30 meeting of the editorial board.

I get the morning papers.

Occasionally, it's back to the drawing board.

The Philadelphia Inquirer

NO NEWS TODAY

EVERTHING THAT DID HAPPEN WAS BORING

HO-HUM

Hope is not lost, however. I go to my office at the newspaper and get the later editions.

Once conceived, the germ of an idea may go through several phases. For example, this progression was stimulated by the gaps in Nixon's tapes.

At 9:30, armed with whatever we've got, the editorial writers and I go to meet the editor.

I have a stimulating and rewarding relationship with my editor. When we disagree about the validity of a cartoon I have proposed, we discuss it in an adult manner.

Occasionally, it's back to the drawing board.

Once I know what I'm going to do, I re-draw the rough, trying to maintain the spontaneity while strengthening the drawing for reproduction.

1973

When the drawing is finished, I take it to the engraver, who photographs it and makes an engraving from the negative.

The engraver isn't alone in not understanding some of my drawings. I used a metaphor, 'the sorcerer's apprentice,' in this cartoon about nuclear waste and proliferation, which many people did not recognize. I spent the whole day on the phone explaining it to people.

With the day's drawing done, I turn my attention to the fan mail.

> *To the Editor:*
>
> *Concerning the* National Observer *note that "Auth grew up in Southern California, a sickly child . . ." you must know by now that he still has not grown up and is even more a sickly child . . . in the head!*
>
> *You will do him and the* Inquirer *a service if you will see that Auth receives urgently needed mental health care by calling the West Philadelphia Mental Health Consortium (BA 2 5583) for an appointment.*

11/28/73

"AUTH"
Editorial Cartoonist
Inquirer
Phila., Penna.

Dear Sir, or It, or Whatever You are:

You are putting out some cartoons ridiculing our President,
                and others
his Secretary/ in a very nasty, slimy manner.

I don't know who you are, or what you are, but I do know that

you are a real creep, who deserves a type of letter such

as this.

                Uncordially,

                P. Foley
                P. Foley

11/28/73

TO TONY AUTH

Here's a good idea for The Inquirer.
It's a picture of Nixon riding naked
on a bike (streaking). Do another
picture so it will look more like him;
I'm just giving you an Idea. Don't
forget to make him naked. You should
write underneath "let me make
one thing perfectly clear."
                aaron

(AS DICTATED TO HIS MOTHER)

Occasionally a young person visits me to talk about a career as an editorial cartoonist.

Sometimes I give lectures.

Sometimes I sleep in the sun.

Here are some of the cartoons I have done in the past five years that have pleased me most:

Holidays are rich in emotional content and symbolism.

There will be six hours of football on television Christmas Day.

—News Item

12/24/71

President Nixon follows Johnson's war policies.

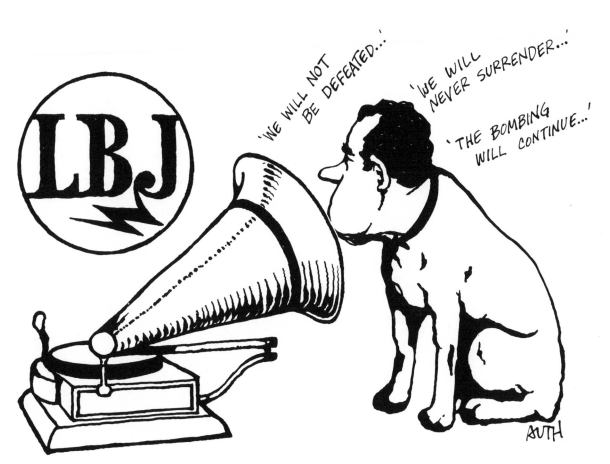

His Master's Voice

4/28/72

The Watergate cover-up begins.

AUTH

WATERGATE
INVESTIGATION

JUSTICE
DEPT.

JUSTICE
DEPT.

7/5/72

The President is re-nominated.

AUTH

8/23/72

The bombing of North Vietnam continues.

North Vietnam bombed military targets in New York City today, in an attempt to force the U. S. to seriously negotiate.

—Imaginary News Item

1/11/73

Inflation becomes an issue.

Melvin Laird, the Secretary of Defense, actually said this.

'If the President was involved, I think full disclosure would be bad. I don't want to know.'
—Melvin Laird

5/4/73

The President's defense.

AUTH

NIXON

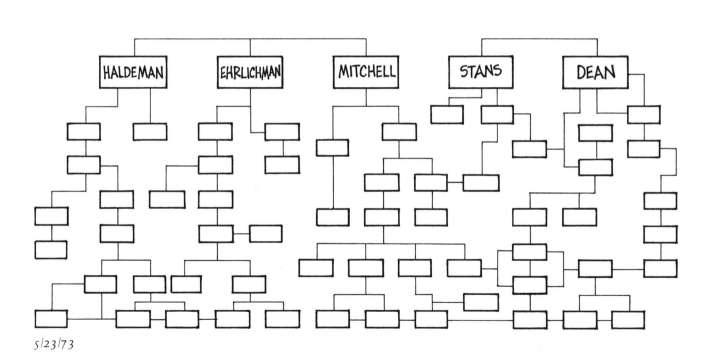

5/23/73

John Dean testifies before the Senate Watergate Committee and accuses the President.

DEAN'S LIST

7/1/73

AUTH

Alexander Butterfield makes known the existence of the White House taping system.

AUTH

7/18/73

The Vice President is in trouble, but Nixon says he supports him.

9/30/73

Agnew resigns, pleading nolo contendere to charges of tax evasion and bribery.

LAW 'N' ORDER

NIXON - AGNEW

AUTH

10/11/73

In the meantime, Kissinger promises that with detente, we can all feel more secure.

AUTH

Detente

10/21/73

Nixon fires the Attorney General and the Assistant Attorney General for refusing to fire the Special Prosecutor, who is then fired by the Solicitor General in the 'Saturday Night Massacre,' which clarifies the President's position.

'Let me make this perfectly clear . . .'

10/23/73

Surprise! There are gaps in Nixon's tapes.

11/25/73

Who do you suppose erased the tapes? Perhaps Rose Mary Woods did it by accident.

11/30/73

ROSE MARY WOODS

AUTH

Meanwhile, the energy crisis intensifies. Almost everyone wonders how much oil we really have.

A panel of experts says that the famous eighteen-and-a-half-minute gap is the result of at least five separate erasures. General Haig, White House Chief of Staff, assures us that nothing important has been erased and blames 'a sinister force.'

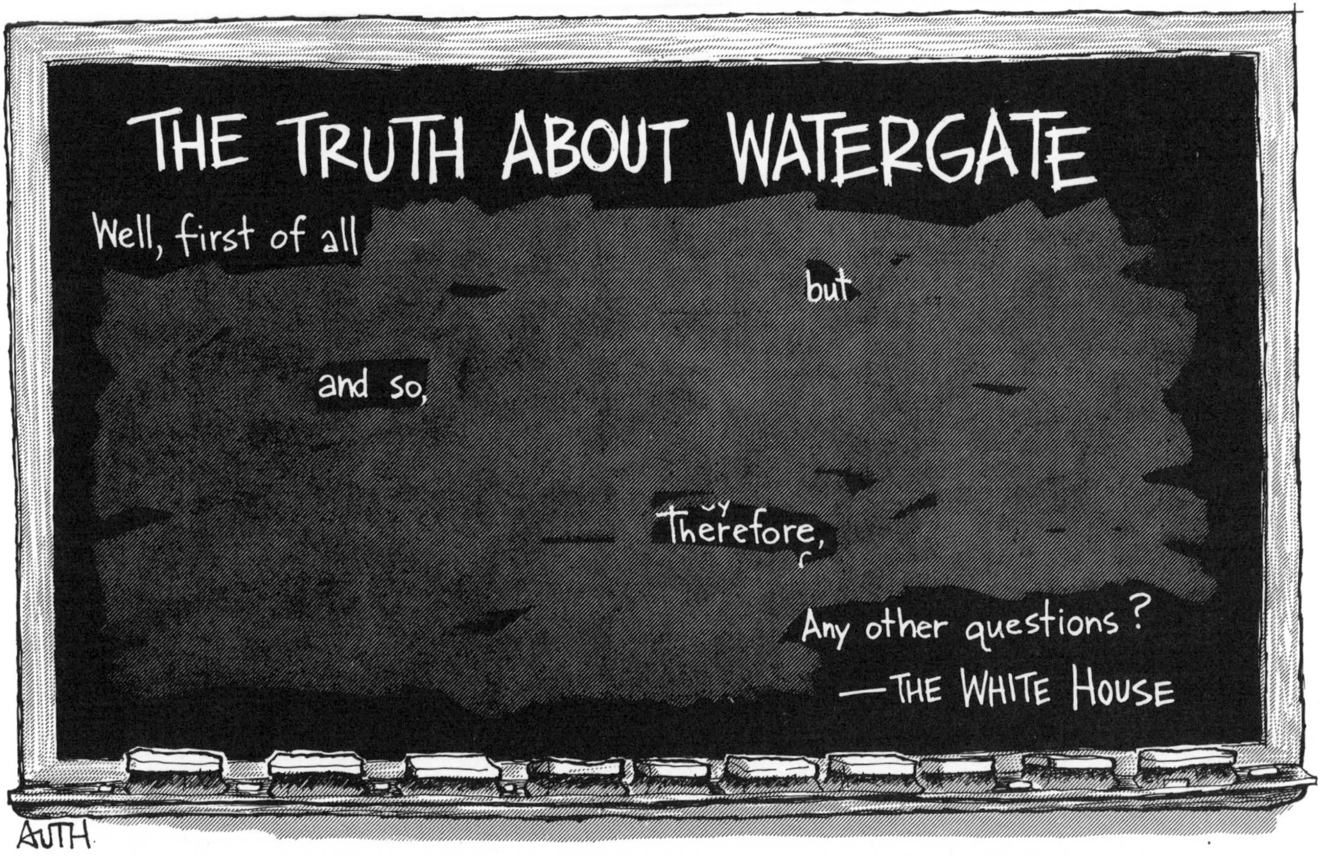
THE TRUTH ABOUT WATERGATE
Well, first of all
but
and so,
Therefore,
Any other questions?
—THE WHITE HOUSE
AUTH
1/17/74

Ah, the burdens of our domestic and foreign policies.

2/20/74

Admiral Moorer, Chairman of the Joint Chiefs of Staff, admits spying on Henry Kissinger in the White House.

2/22/74

After trying hard not to, Nixon is forced to release transcripts of some of his tapes.

5/10/74

Nixon turns scholar.

'According to my research, only 3 Americans could have been impeached if they'd been President. Benedict Arnold, Al Capone, and the Boston Strangler.'

6/2/74

Kissinger gets very angry when he is accused of being involved in some illegal wiretapping. The Congress passes a resolution stating that Kissinger is a great man who travels about the world in search of peace.

AUTH

6/14/74

'May I have your autograph, please . . .'

6/28/74

The President also travels, and visits the Soviet Union.

WELCOME TO MOSCOW

AUTH

6/25/74

The White House releases the 'smoking gun' tapes of June 23, 1972. The President announces his resignation the following day.

'I cannot tell the truth . . .'

8/8/74

Ford enters the White House, with almost everybody wishing him well.

AUTH

8/10/74

A lot of people don't like the Vietnam War. Many dodge the draft. Some admit it.

Pick the draft dodger.

HE FEIGNED ILLNESS.

HE TOOK DRUGS THAT RAISED HIS BLOOD PRESSURE.

AUTH

HE STAYED IN SCHOOL 12 YRS.

HE GOT MARRIED.

HE PRETENDED TO BE GAY.

HE OBJECTED TO THE WAR ON MORAL GROUNDS AND WENT TO CANADA.

9/18/74

The U.S suffers at the hands of the Arab oil producers.

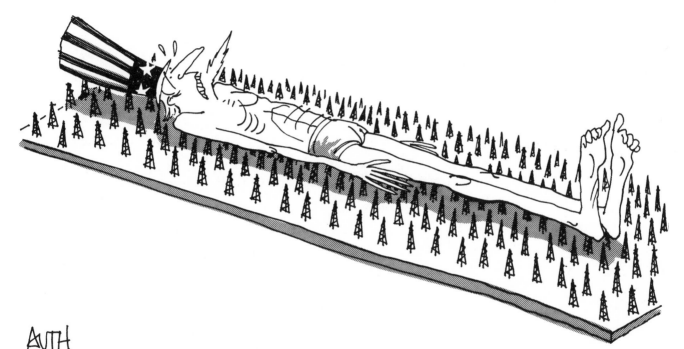

When the Democrats are overwhelmingly elected in the '74 congressional elections, the press, saying 'The Democrats have the ball,' asks 'What will they do with it?'

11/8/74

The food-exporting countries of the world hold a conference to decide how to equitably distribute the world's food . . . and disagree.

After issuing conflicting statements about whether a tax increase or a tax cut is what's needed for the economy, the
President goes off to ski in Vail, Colorado.

TAX INCREASE

TAX CUT

AUTH

12/26/74

Meanwhile . . .

'The wages of sin are fantastic!'

1/24/75

People begin looking forward to 1976.

'What are we planning for the Bicentennial?'

With détente in trouble, much is made of the joint Soviet and American space mission.

AUTH

7/15/75

The F.B.I. admits committing thousands of burglaries.

'That's the burglar! The one in the suit!'

7/17/75

The heroes of Soviet agriculture turn out to live in Kansas.

'O beautiful for spacious skies
For amber waves of grain . . .'

7/22/75

Betty Ford says she would not be shocked if her daughter had an affair.

Nixon agrees, for a very large sum of money, to 'tell all.'

"David Frost here with 'Let's Make a Deal', 'To Tell the Truth', and 'The Price is Right'."

8/17/75

Peace-loving Americans love their guns.

9/16/75

Americans in other parts of the country respond to New York City in its time of need.

A ferocious civil war rages in Lebanon, with the population divided along religious lines.

10/30/75

We discover that the F.B.I. waged a surreptitious campaign against Martin Luther King, Jr. One blackmail threat hinted he ought to commit suicide.

'We've got to get Martin Luther King, Jr. . . . he's positively un-American!'

11/20/75

The federal government comes through with aid to New York City.

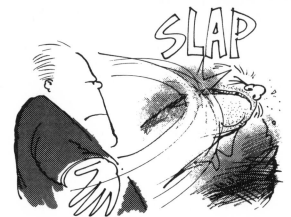

Judith Campbell Exner cashes in on her alleged affair with JFK.

AUTH
1/16/76

Americans pull out all the stops for their country's 200th birthday.

'In what other country are the people free enough to do
this to their Bicentennial?'

2/5/76

In the middle of our presidential primaries, Richard Nixon accepts an invitation to visit his old friends in China.

'It's from a Richard Nixon. He's donating a report on China to the State Department and taking a $100,000 deduction.'

3/4/76

Time marches on, and the clock is running out in Africa.

'Guess who's coming to dinner . . .'

3/26/76

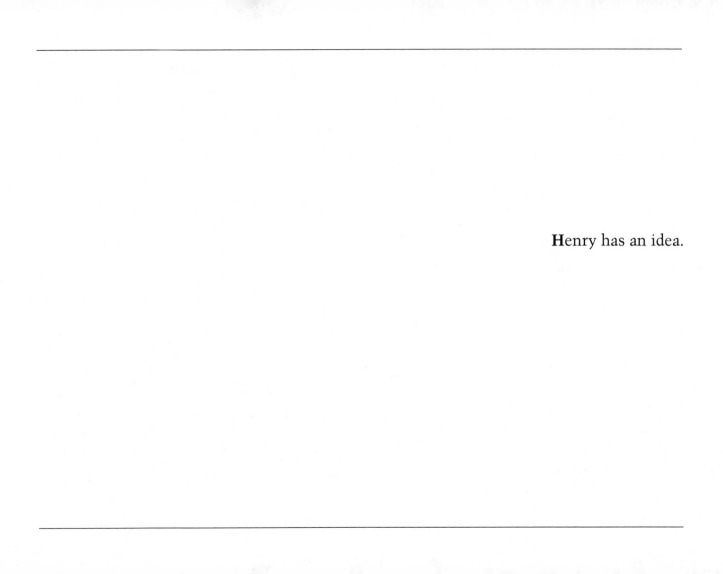

Henry has an idea.

AFRICA

AUTH

4/27/76

Congressman Wayne Hays maintained his mistress on the federal payroll.

July 4, 1976.

The Israelis rescue over 100 hijacked hostages from terrorists at Uganda's Entebbe Airport.

AUTH

7/7/76

Jimmy Carter, peanut farmer from Georgia, wins the Democratic nomination for President.

AUTH

7/18/76

Viking 1 lands on Mars and samples the soil.

VIKING 1

AUTH

7/29/76

On June 7, 1976, officials of Hatfield Borough, Pennsylvania, notified Jonathan Selby, 29, that he would have to tear down the tree house he had built in his back yard. Mr. Selby was accused of not applying for a building permit and of exceeding the 40-foot height restriction. Selby defied the authorities, and on July 28, two Borough police cars, a Montgomery County sheriff's cruiser, a dump truck, and a power line truck with a cherry picker converged on the tree house and destroyed it.

MR SELBY

AUTH
7/30/76

Amnesty for Vietnam draft evaders and deserters is still an issue.

The back-alley butchers rejoice.

FEDERAL FUNDS DENIED FOR MOST ABORTIONS

MEDICAL DICTIONARY

AUTH

9/20/76

The first televised presidential debates since 1960.

AUTH

9/21/76

MILLIONS
APATHETIC

During one of his debates with Carter, President Ford says that Eastern Europe is not dominated by the Soviet Union.

'President Ford declared our independence. Pass it on.'

10/7/76

Election day.

11/2/76

Jimmy Carter is elected President.

'Okay, bring in the new guy . . .'

11/4/76

It is announced that Amy will attend public school.

AUTH
11/30/76

Often on the way home, I think of a slight change, an added touch that would have made that day's drawing much better.

At home at night, I relax.   Tomorrow's a new day.

Auth began his career as a cartoonist in California where he drew weekly cartoons for OPEN CITY, a Los Angeles anti-war underground weekly. In 1971 he was hired as staff editorial cartoonist for THE PHILADELPHIA INQUIRER where his work appears five times a week. His drawings are distributed internationally by The Washington Post Writers Group. He has won almost every national award for cartooning, including the Overseas Press Club Award, the Sigma Delta Chi Award, and, in 1976, the Pulitzer Prize.